Thirty
TRUTHS
for Common Lies

—

FOR WOMEN

ALEXA HESS

When the enemy whispers lies to us, we can combat them with the truth of God's Word.

Table of CONTENTS

There are moments when we are going about our everyday lives, and a thought pierces our minds. *You aren't good enough. You don't matter. Other people are more liked than you.* Often, but not always, certain events will trigger these lies. For example, when we mess up at work, yell at our kids, or forget to do something important, these thoughts may enter in without our permission. Or perhaps other people have spoken lies to us. They are the ones who tell us, "You are not good enough," "You do not matter," or "Other people are more liked than you." When we dwell on lies, whether spoken to us or existing within our minds, we can start to believe these words are true. If we choose to accept these lies rather than fight against them, we can find our self-worth crushed, our faith tested, and our purpose questioned.

Why do we believe lies? Why is it so easy to buy into the false words that are spoken to us and enter our minds? We believe lies because of sin. When God created the world, He proclaimed all of creation good. Not one part of God's creation was imperfect or evil. Humans experienced what it was like to walk with God and live with a mind and body that were at peace. While Adam and Eve were free to eat from any tree in the garden, they were not allowed to eat from the Tree of Knowledge of Good and Evil. As long as Adam and Eve obeyed this command, they would continue to delight in the abundance of the creation and their Creator.

But one day, Satan took the form of a serpent and approached Eve, tempting her to eat the fruit from this forbidden tree. Satan questioned God's command to Adam and Eve and even refuted God's words. Satan told Eve, "No! You will certainly not die.... In fact, God knows that when you eat it your eyes will be opened and you will be like God, knowing good and evil" (Genesis 3:4–5). Satan tempted Eve to doubt God's command and believe that God was withholding good from her by His command. Sadly, Eve believed the lie of the serpent and ate the fruit. Adam, too, took the fruit and ate it, and through their disobedience, sin entered the world.

Sin clouds our judgment and causes us to believe the deceiver rather than the God of truth. Without a relationship with God, our eyes are blinded, and our ears are blocked from receiving truth. On our own, we are defenseless to rid ourselves of the sin that entangles us and come back to the God we deny. But out of His abundant grace and mercy, God sent us Jesus, who is full of grace and truth (John 1:14). Jesus took the punishment we deserve for our sin by dying on the cross; three days later, Jesus rose from the dead, declaring His power over sin and death.

When we repent of our sin and trust in Jesus, we receive forgiveness for our sin. The grace of Jesus opens our eyes and ears, uniting us with the God of truth. Through God's Word, we can be people who walk in truth and lead others to the gospel's truth. However, while Jesus gives us a redeemed heart, we still have a sinful nature and a very present enemy on this side of eternity. Daily, we will battle against the lies Satan places in our minds. But we do not have to succumb to the lies of the enemy or the lies of sinful mankind. As followers of Christ, we have the Holy Spirit inside of us who helps us fight against lies. Through the power of the Spirit, we can resist the father of lies and rest in our heavenly Father, who speaks truth over us. As believers, we have the Spirit and God's Word. When the enemy whispers lies to us, we can combat them with the truth of God's Word.

In this booklet, we will walk through thirty everyday lies we often hear or even tell ourselves. We will tackle each lie with the truth of Scripture and be reminded of what is true in Christ. We will learn how to speak truth over ourselves when lies invade, and we will begin to recognize the habits of thought that cause us to be deceived. Most of all, we will learn how we can fight against everyday lies and rest in the God of truth through the power of God's Word.

Editors' Note: This booklet was written with the intent of helping you apply biblical truth to lies you may believe. Some of these lies may apply to you, and some may not, based on where you live, your culture, your personal struggles, or any number of factors. However, through this resource, we hope you will find truth to combat whatever lies are impacting you.

BE IN GOD'S WORD DAILY

We need to regularly be in God's Word to know God's truth. If we remove ourselves from God's Word, we leave ourselves vulnerable in the moments lies strike. Without the regular reminder of the truths of God's Word, we can easily buy into the lies we hear and see. Make it a priority to be in God's Word daily so that you can learn what is true and rest in truth.

MEMORIZE SCRIPTURE

Along with regularly reading God's Word, we can memorize what God's Word says. Memorizing Scripture helps us call to mind God's truth when lies arise. You can combat lies by speaking these memorized truths over yourself. You can choose verses to memorize from your own personal time of Bible study, or you can consider choosing some of the verses listed in this booklet to memorize. Here are three methods for Scripture memorization:

1. Say the verse aloud, and repeat each part several times.

2. Write out the verse over and over on a piece of paper.

3. Follow the letter method by writing the first letter of each word in the verse and memorizing the word that accompanies that letter. For example, you would write out T T I N N C F T I C J to help you memorize, "Therefore, there is now no condemnation for those in Christ Jesus" (Romans 8:1).

03 PRAY

When lies strike, you can ask the Lord to remind you of His truth. You can ask for God's voice to be louder than the lies and for Him to help you cling to what is true. You can also ask God to give you discernment to know whether something is true or not. It can be hard at times to know if something you read or see is true, but you can ask God to give you the wisdom to distinguish between lies and truth.

04 SHARE WITH OTHERS

God has given us our fellow believers to help shoulder our burdens. If you are struggling with certain lies, share this struggle with a trusted friend, pastor, or counselor. Talking through lies you are wrestling with allows others to speak truth into your life. Sharing this with your community also allows your brothers and sisters in Christ the opportunity to point out lies that you perhaps weren't even aware you were believing.

OUR POWERLESSNESS
IS MEANT TO LEAD US TO
THE GOD WHOSE POWER
NEVER RUNS DRY.

01

LIE:

I can operate in my own strength

We tend to operate in our own strength more than we realize. As sinful people, our natural inclination is to be the ones in control. We like to be the ones who call the shots and check off as many boxes on our to-do lists as possible. Yet we encounter burnout, failures, and frustrations. The restlessness we experience, the mistakes we make, and the weaknesses we possess show not only that we cannot truly operate in our own strength but that we were never supposed to operate in our own strength anyway. Our powerlessness is meant to lead us to the God whose power never runs dry.

However, even with the knowledge that we cannot operate in our own strength and need the strength of God, we still may resist God's help. We may push off coming to God in prayer and asking for His strength. We may neglect to rest in the power of the Holy Spirit inside of us. Choosing to operate in this way only perpetuates burnout and frustration in our lives. It is when we accept the fact that we cannot operate in our strength and we turn to the Lord that we will experience rest and the ability to do the work He has called us to do.

It can be hard to admit our weakness, especially living in this world. Our world praises strength and puts down those who are weak and make mistakes. But, as believers, we have a unique opportunity to showcase God's glory when we choose to rely on God's strength. When we admit our weaknesses, we create an opportunity for ourselves and others to witness God's strength powerfully working within us.

Paul writes in 2 Corinthians 4:7, "Now we have this treasure in clay jars, so that this extraordinary power may be from God and not from us." This means God uses our weaknesses and inabilities to intentionally showcase His glory. When we

"God uses our weaknesses and inabilities to intentionally showcase His glory."

embrace the reality of our insufficiencies rather than fight against our insufficiencies, we proclaim to the world God's extraordinary power. Instead of looking at our weaknesses and frailties with contempt, we can be like Paul, who chose to boast all the more about his weakness so that Christ's power would reside in him (2 Corinthians 12:9). After all, we were never meant to be the ones to receive glory, for God created us to showcase His glory.

Therefore, instead of ignoring God's power, let us admit our weaknesses and accept the reality that without the Lord, we cannot do anything. Let us rely on and rest in the strength of the God who graciously empowers us. This will be a daily battle, for we will have to continuously fight against our tendency to operate in our own power. But, as we keep turning to God in prayer and asking for His help, we will surrender our control and rest in the power of the Lord. You cannot operate in your own power, which is a good thing. So embrace your insufficiencies, and turn to your all-sufficient God, who supplies you with His strength.

ACTION STEP

Consider one or two areas of your life where you need to actively lean on God's strength rather than your own.

LIE:

I am a burden to others

The lie that we are a burden to others can often enter our minds because of the limitations we possess. Maybe we have a physical disorder that prevents us from being able to participate in important family events and opportunities. Maybe we live with a disability that requires someone to care for our basic needs or drive us to different places. Maybe we experience mental battles that affect the relationships around us. Whatever we feel the burden may be, it can be easy for this lie to spring up in our minds.

The lie that we are a burden to others is a lie the enemy loves to perpetuate. The enemy can fuel this lie as a way to encourage us to retreat from others and pull us into isolation. The enemy can also use this thought to cause us to become bitter with God about our weaknesses and sufferings. Believing the lie that we are a burden to others can leave us incredibly distraught and even depressed. Instead of succumbing to this thought, we can rest in this important truth from Scripture: We are not a burden to others because God uses others to help carry our burdens.

Galatians 6:2 says, "Carry one another's burdens; in this way you will fulfill the law of Christ." This is not a simple encouragement but a command. As followers of Christ, we are commanded to carry the burdens of others willingly and joyfully. This command reveals how God has graciously given us other people to come alongside us and help us. While God supplies His help, strength, and power daily, He also works through others to come to our aid. The burdens we experience are not meant to be carried alone. By His grace, God places people in our lives to shoulder the heavy load of our sufferings and weaknesses.

Therefore, people are a gift to us in our moments and seasons of pain. Instead of viewing ourselves as a burden because of our needs, we can be reminded of how others show their love for us as they take care of us. This love is a mere fraction of the love God has for us. In His infinite love, God chose to send His Son to die for us on the cross. Jesus willingly carried the burden of our sin and shame on the cross and allowed this burden to crush Him in death. But three days later, Jesus rose from the dead, declaring His victory not only over the burden of sin—but every burden sin creates. As people carry our burdens, we are reminded of our Savior, who says to us, "Come to me, all of you who are weary and burdened, and I will give you rest" (Matthew 11:28).

Just because you carry burdens does not mean you are a burden to others. Our burdens themselves may cause strain as others help to carry them, but it is the burdens themselves that are weighty, not the person who is experiencing them. May God's Word remind you that you are not a burden for having limitations and needing the help of others. Even if your burdens are heavy, you are gifted both the strength of others and the strength of God to lift your every weight.

ACTION STEP

Consider a couple of ways that others are currently showing love to you through their actions.

03

LIE:

What has happened to me defines me

99

Many of us experience painful events that impact our lives greatly, whether the event may be a difficult childhood, an instance of trauma, or a situation of assault. Our past hurts come with us like baggage we never intended to carry. When something happens to us that is outside of our control, we can be left feeling broken, afraid, and maybe even worthless. The painful situations we have walked through can cause us to believe the lie that what has happened to us defines our self-worth and perhaps even who we are as a person overall.

The truth of Scripture heavily combats the idea that past hurts are tied to our self-worth. God's Word tells us that what has happened to us does not define us—who we are in Christ defines us. Second Corinthians 5:17 says, "Therefore, if anyone is in Christ, he is a new creation; the old has passed away, and see, the new has come!" To say the old has passed away does not mean that what has happened to us is now wiped from our past and memory. What it does mean is that the sinful self we possessed before coming to Christ has been replaced with a new, redeemed self.

When we come to faith in Christ, we are no longer defined by our sin but by the grace of Christ. But what does this mean for sin that has been done to us? This means that when we come to Christ, Christ's grace heals the brokenness of our past. While we will still be reminded of what has happened to us and may still struggle to work through the thoughts and emotions triggered by the past, our salvation declares that though we feel broken, we are made whole in Christ.

The beautiful truth of our salvation is the fact that what has happened to us through Christ is what defines us for

"When we come to Christ, Christ's grace heals the brokenness of our past."

the rest of our lives. When we come to faith in Christ, we are declared redeemed. Christ's grace cleanses our past, present, and future. We are declared justified. We stand before the Father completely innocent because of Christ's sacrifice. We are adopted into an eternal family and declared a child of God. These truths are what define our personhood and self-worth. And the best part about these truths is that they will never be taken away. What has happened to you or what may happen to you in the future cannot rob you of your identity in Christ.

As we rest in who we are in Christ, we also rest in what He will do when He returns. One day, Christ will return to remove sin once and for all. He will punish all wickedness and set right every wrong. This means that the painful events of our past will be completely removed. Our minds and bodies will be renewed so that never again will we sin or be sinned against. With the presence of sin removed, we will know no brokenness or pain.

When the events of your past threaten your self-worth, remember who you are in Christ. Your salvation in Christ and your status in the kingdom of God is what defines you now and for all eternity.

─────────── ACTION STEP ───────────

Using the space provided on the next page, journal about how the hope of the gospel and the hope of eternity impact your self-worth.

*The hope of the gospel and the hope of
eternity impact my self-worth.*

WE WERE NOT CREATED TO
PLACE OUR IDENTITY IN THE
PERCEPTIONS OF OTHERS.

LIE:

People think I am _____

When you read the title of this lie, how do you finish the sentence? Maybe you feel as if people think you are unattractive, unintelligent, boring, or weak. Maybe you think people view you as too much, too loud, or too quiet. Whatever your answer may be, this thought often enters our minds when we interact with others or when a certain circumstance involving others occurs. For example, if we stumble over our words in a job interview or presentation, we may worry that people are zeroing in on our weaknesses. Or, if we walk into a room with people who look very different from us, we may worry that they are picking out our flaws or insecurities.

Focusing on others' perceptions is rooted in our fear of man. When we fear man, we allow how others view us to define us and influence us. The truth is, what we think others believe about us is most often not even true at all. We are the ones assuming the negative perceptions of others.

But what about when someone else finishes the lie in the title? What if they say that we are unintelligent, unattractive, or too much? This, too, involves the fear of man. When we fear man, the words and opinions of others hold more weight than God's Word.

While there are times when we should listen to the words of others, especially if they involve a sin issue in our lives, we were not created to place our identity in the perceptions of others. God created us to worship and glorify Him. But when we focus more on what others think or say than what God says, we elevate man over God. In essence, we worship the opinions and perceptions of others when we care more about people's responses than glorifying God. Proverbs 29:25 tells us, "The fear of mankind is a snare, but the one who trusts in the Lord is protected." The fear of mankind snares us because, like an animal stuck in a trap, we cannot be freed from people's hold over our lives in our own strength.

We fight the fear of man by fearing the Lord most of all. Instead of fixating on the perceptions of others, we are to focus on worshiping God and being faithful to Him. When we fear the Lord, our gaze will be focused upward at the God of glory instead of downward at flawed mankind. Focusing our attention on pleasing the Lord over pleasing man also reminds us of what is true for us in Christ. When we worship God, we are reminded that we are loved by our heavenly Father (John 15:9), that we receive grace for our weaknesses (2 Corinthians 12:9), and that we are remarkably and wondrously made (Psalm 139:14).

In addition to worshiping the Lord, we must remain rooted in the truth of God's Word. We are to let Scripture frame and determine our identity, not the thoughts and opinions of others. Worshiping the Lord and resting in the truth of Scripture keeps our identity in Christ alone. When our identity is in Christ, the thoughts and opinions of others will not sway us. Instead, we will remain secure in who we are in Christ and who God's Word declares us to be.

ACTION STEP

List out three truths declaring who you are in Christ that you can recall and rest in when this lie enters your mind.

LIE:

I am a failure

Each day, we fail in one way or another. As imperfect humans, it is impossible to do everything perfectly. Yet, even though we know this truth, we can still become down on ourselves when we fail. As our awareness of our failures grows, it can be easy to deem ourselves failures. Dwelling on the lie that we are our failures can be extremely discouraging. This lie can make us give up on our work or responsibilities or even cause us to believe that we will never amount to anything.

While moments of failure are difficult, moments of failure do not have to be debilitating. But how then can we remain secure even in moments of failure? When we rest in Christ's grace, Jesus gives us His grace for our every failure. Our God knows that we are imperfect people and will make mistakes. Even still, God's love for us remains steady, and His grace overflows to us no matter how many times we fail. If we doubt this truth, all we have to do is look to the story of Scripture. All throughout the Bible, we find example after example of people who failed. God's chosen people, the Israelites, constantly failed in their obedience and faithfulness to God. The leaders and kings God chose, such as Moses and David, failed in their leadership and personal integrity. But God never gave up on His people, though they failed Him over and over again.

God's steadfastness to remain committed to His people is displayed most brilliantly at the cross. God demonstrated His great love for us by the sacrifice of Christ. Through the death and resurrection of Jesus, we receive God's forgiveness and grace that covers all of our sins, shortcomings, and imperfections. And the beautiful reality of God's grace is

"Because of Christ, God does not look at us as failures but as redeemed people."

that it never runs dry. Like those in the Bible, we too will fail in our lives and our relationship with God, but God's grace remains steadfast. Because of Christ, God does not look at us as failures but as redeemed people.

Knowing that our God forgives our failures and does not fault us for them allows us to feel at peace when we experience mishaps. Not only this, but moments of failure also become opportunities to rest in Christ's strength. Second Corinthians 12:9 says, "But he said to me, 'My grace is sufficient for you, for my power is perfected in weakness.'" When we fail, we can admit our weakness and our inability to be perfect, and we can turn to Jesus, who gives us His strength. We do not have the strength in and of ourselves to pick ourselves up when we stumble and fall. But in Christ, we have a strong and steady hand that lifts us and helps us to keep going. Psalm 37:24 tells us, "Though he falls, he will not be overwhelmed, because the Lord supports him with his hand." God gives us His grace for our stumblings and His strength to persevere.

Failure is inevitable, but we have a God whose mercies are new every morning. May we not view ourselves as failures but as redeemed children, loved and aided by our heavenly Father, for this is our true identity.

ACTION STEP

Memorize a Bible verse that you can recall in the moments you feel like a failure.

06

LIE:

My worth is determined by what I do and how I do it

The lie that our worth is determined by what we do and how we do it is a lie our culture fuels. There is a well-known phrase that says, "You are what you do." We can see how this is a common belief through the way we communicate with one another. One of the first questions we often ask when meeting someone is, "What do you do?" We are also accustomed to identifying ourselves by what we do, whether we are mothers, teachers, or leaders. While it is not wrong to use such identifiers for ourselves, it can be harmful to allow what we do to become our ultimate identity. When what we do becomes our ultimate identity, how we go about what we do can determine how we view ourselves.

This is why we often criticize or become frustrated with ourselves when we make mistakes. We can think, *I'm a terrible mom because I forgot to pick my child up from school,* or *I did not do as good of a job as another on a project; what is wrong with me?* When we allow our self-worth to be determined by what we do and how we do it, we set ourselves up to be disappointed and extremely insecure. Not only this, but if whatever it is we are placing our identity in is taken away, we can be left feeling broken and hopeless. If we lose our jobs or our role as parents, we can wonder, *Who am I?*

Our world may say that we are what we do, but the gospel says otherwise. The gospel declares that we are not defined by what we do but by what Christ has done for us. The salvation we receive through Christ's death and resurrection is our main source of identity (Romans 8:17, 2 Corinthians 5:17–18). This truth is incredibly freeing because it takes the pressure off of ourselves to perform perfectly or achieve a favorable result. Because our identity is rooted in Christ, we remain secure no matter what we do or what

"The identities of this world will all fade away, but who we are in Christ prevails."

mistakes we make. This means that even if our roles shift or are removed, who we are in Christ remains.

When our identity is in Christ, how we see ourselves will not be determined by our successes or failures, and our security will not be rooted in what we do. Instead of a worldly identity, our identity will come from these truths of Scripture: I am a child of God, I am chosen, I am forgiven, I am made new. These truths remain no matter the positions we hold or lose.

There will still be moments when the world may judge us for what we do and what we accomplish. There will still be times when we are tempted to shame ourselves for our failures or weaknesses. Nevertheless, we can remain confident and at peace as we rest in Christ. The identities of this world will all fade away, but who we are in Christ prevails. Therefore, may we choose to rest in who we are in Christ above our roles and abilities.

—— ACTION STEP ——

Think of one practical way you can rest in Christ and who you are in Him when this lie enters your mind.

THE GRACE AND POWER OF
JESUS PROVIDE US WITH TRUE
AND LASTING CHANGE.

LIE:

I cannot change

07

"No matter our weaknesses, God will see His work of sanctification through in our lives."

Most of us have something about ourselves that we would like to change. While some of these things may be minor, we can also desire change in a much grander way. Maybe there is a sin struggle or a bad habit we cannot overcome. Whatever it may be, trying to make a big change can be daunting and discouraging. We may start with a burst of motivation to change and even experience progress, only to then plummet into despair when we fail. The difficulties that come with change can cause us to throw up our hands in frustration and believe the lie that there is no way we can change.

The truth is, we cannot change in our own power; change is only possible through Christ. The grace and power of Jesus provide us with true and lasting change. Christ's forgiveness washes away our sin and replaces our old and sinful hearts with new and redeemed hearts.

However, our renewed hearts are not the only change we experience when we come to know Christ. God changes us through the power of the Holy Spirit into the image of Christ. This process of sanctification is a lifelong process that is finished when one day we stand glorified before God. Until then, God is slowly transforming us, from one degree of glory to another, into the image of His Son (2 Corinthians 3:18).

While God can do a powerful work in our lives and change us quickly, the process of sanctification is often slow. Even still, Philippians 1:6 tells us, "I am sure of this, that he who started a good work in you will carry it on to completion until the day of Christ Jesus." No matter our weaknesses, God will see His work of sanctification through in our lives. Though we may fail in our efforts to change, it is God's pow-

34

er and grace that transforms us. Therefore, to say that we cannot change is to discredit the power of God that works within us. We are helpless on our own, but with the power of Christ, we can change.

It is incredibly freeing to know that we need the power of God in order to change. If the ability to change required our efforts alone, we would be continuously disappointed. But, because God is the One who ultimately produces growth in our lives, we can be encouraged. In the moments when change feels out of reach, we can remember how God is the One who works within us. We can be confident, knowing that God will move us forward no matter our stumbles and struggles.

While ultimate change is not possible on this side of eternity, we can be comforted by resting in our glorification to come. One day, all the struggles and sins we battle will be removed. God will complete His work of sanctification in us, and we will be given new selves with no spot or stain. Until that day comes, we can rest in the power of God. Through the power of the Spirit, we can rely on His strength to push through the obstacles we face in the process of growth. We cannot change by our own strength, so may we trust in the strength of the Lord.

--- ACTION STEP ---

Take a moment to consider your habits. What are one or two habits you can change with God's help?

08

LIE:

What I am doing is meaningless

Perhaps you are working a 9–5 job that feels mundane. You clock into work and clock back out later thinking, *Did anything I did today matter?* Or maybe you are in a position or role you have worked hard to accomplish or always dreamed of having, only to be left wondering if what you are doing carries any weight. It can be easy to believe the lie that what we are doing is meaningless because we cannot always see what our work is accomplishing. There is not always visible evidence that what we are doing is actually benefiting anything or anyone. But, even though we may feel as if what we are doing is meaningless, everything we do has meaning if we are in Christ.

God created us to worship Him, and He even created work as an opportunity to glorify Him. Sin now distorts our worship and causes us to seek glory in ourselves instead. But when we enter into a relationship with Christ, Jesus's grace makes us new. While we still struggle against our sinful nature, our new and redeemed hearts delight in serving the Lord and giving Him glory. Because of Christ, everything we do is a work of service unto the Lord. Colossians 3:23–25 says, "Whatever you do, do it from the heart, as something done for the Lord and not for people, knowing that you will receive the reward of an inheritance from the Lord. You serve the Lord Christ." When our hearts are focused on Christ, what we do has meaning because what we do brings glory to the Lord.

What we do is also meaningful because our labor has kingdom significance. God has called each one of us to a certain

> "There is no place or position God has called us to that He does not use for His kingdom's purposes."

place or position, not only to give Him glory but to build His kingdom. Through the power of the Spirit, God works through what we do to build His kingdom on earth as it is in heaven. However, the enemy wants us to forget this important truth. He tries to make us believe the lie that what we do is meaningless to keep us from doing what God has called us to do. When we buy into the enemy's schemes, we are prevented from being the kingdom builders God has called us to be. Instead of listening to his lies, we must remember that each of us has an important role in expanding God's kingdom. There is no place or position God has called us to that He does not use for His kingdom's purposes.

While there will be times when we will still struggle to see the fruit of our efforts, all that we do will be worthwhile when we stand before the Lord and hear the words, "Well done, good and faithful servant" (Matthew 25:21, 23). May these future words cause us to take up what God has called us to do with joy and perseverance in the present. Let the impact of our efforts encourage us to work hard, even in moments of frustration and weariness. Let the knowledge that our work gives God glory fill us with delight.

Because of Christ, everything we do has meaning, so may we work heartily unto the One who moves in and through us.

ACTION STEP

Think of one way you can change your attitude about a seemingly mundane or unimportant task and instead view that task as an opportunity to glorify God.

09

LIE:

I am a bad parent or spouse

99

We lose patience with our spouses and yell at them. Our child's teacher calls us to tell us we forgot to pack our child's lunch. Moments of frustration or personal mistakes can cause us to believe that we are bad parents or spouses. But other people can also make us feel this way. Others can pass judgment upon us for our children's behavior or how we go about our marriages.

Often, our failures reveal not that we are bad parents or spouses but broken parents and spouses. The mistakes we make reveal that we are sinners. As sinful and imperfect people, we will fail in our roles as parents and spouses. Yet, instead of turning inwardly at our failures, we can turn upward to the face of Christ. When we look to Jesus, we are reminded how Christ is the One who forgives and heals our brokenness. Therefore, when guilt arises or other people pass judgment, we can rest in the grace of Christ. We can be cheered in remembering that even though we sin, there is no condemnation for those of us in Christ (Romans 8:1). And, if Christ does not speak words of condemnation over us, why should we speak words of condemnation over ourselves?

However, just because there is no condemnation in Christ does not mean we should ignore the conviction we receive through our relationship with Christ. While condemnation accuses us and does not come from the Lord, at times, the Spirit does bring conviction into our hearts to reveal how we may be saying or doing something sinful. Moments of conviction are a good thing as they are opportunities to lean into the work of sanctification God is accomplishing in our lives. If we ignore the Spirit's conviction, we can act in certain ways that are sinful and even harmful toward our spouses or children.

"The Holy Spirit empowers us to keep pursuing righteousness."

As believers, we should strive to listen to the conviction of the Spirit and be quick to confess our sins so that we can continue to grow in Christlikeness.

Instead of growing discouraged and even self-degrading over our sins and imperfections, we can have peace, knowing that we are given help in the pursuit of holiness. When we come to know Christ, we receive the Holy Spirit, who comes to permanently dwell in us. The Holy Spirit helps us fight against our flesh and walk in faithfulness to God. Even though we will fail in our holiness, the Holy Spirit empowers us to keep pursuing righteousness. The grace of Christ and the presence of the Holy Spirit are both deep encouragements to us in the moments we fail. Instead of degrading ourselves for our sins and mistakes, we can remember Christ's grace and rejoice that Christ forgives our failures. And, through the power of the Spirit, we can continue to pursue holiness that helps us be godly parents and spouses.

Obedience and faithfulness to God shape our behaviors and actions. Because obedience to Him matters, we do not have to rely on our own power and abilities to be "good" parents or spouses. As long as we are resting in the grace of Christ and pursuing faithfulness to Him, we will be parents and spouses who reflect Christlikeness.

—————————— ACTION STEP ——————————

Share with another parent or married person about your struggles with this lie.

ULTIMATELY, GOD DISPLAYED
HOW HE IS IN THE BUSINESS
OF CHANGE AND RENEWAL
BY SENDING JESUS.

10

LIE:

My circumstances
will never change

Have you ever been in a season or situation that felt like it would last forever? Perhaps you are in that place right now. These circumstances can be extremely discouraging. Sometimes it can feel as if God has brought you to this place to leave you there. When a certain circumstance does not change, we can easily believe the lie that the situation will never get better.

The way God works in our lives can be frustrating. We do not always understand His plans or why He has allowed certain situations or sufferings. Even still, in His divine sovereignty, God controls the circumstances of our lives for our good and His glory (Romans 8:28). We may not know why God has brought us into certain situations, but we do know that He works through every situation and season—no matter how long they persist. Because God works everything for our good and His glory, we can confidently know that our difficult circumstances will, one day, change.

However, when and how our circumstances change depends on God's sovereign will. He may cause a certain situation to persist more than others for a particular reason that only He knows. In these moments, we can remember how God works through each and every circumstance, even the hard and the painful ones, to shape us into the image of Christ. We may not know the "why" behind the situation God has brought each of us to, but we do know that God is using each situation to transform us into Christlikeness. Therefore, even if the changing of our circumstances feels slow, we can lean into such times and be open-handed, confident that God is sanctifying us in that season.

We can also have hope in lingering circumstances by remembering that God is a God of change. From the very

"We can rest in the truth that God will make all things new."

beginning of Scripture, we learn how God ordered creation by the words of His mouth. He changed the earth from a place of darkness to a place of life and abundance. And even when humans disobeyed God and brought sin into the world, He continued to work in the lives of His people to bring about change. He promised a covenant of restoration, delivered the Israelites from slavery, and even brought His people back from exile. Many of these people had to wait and trust the Lord as He orchestrated His good plan of renewal and restoration, but God was faithful to accomplish His purposes in their lives. Ultimately, God displayed how He is in the business of change and renewal by sending Jesus. Through the death and resurrection of Jesus, those who come to faith in Him have their sins forgiven, their hearts redeemed, and their lives remade.

But God did not cease His work of change after Jesus came. Right here and now, God is orchestrating change through the power of the Spirit as He builds His kingdom on earth. And one day, God will complete His work of change once and for all when He transforms all of creation back into a place of perfect peace. If God has promised to redeem the whole world when He returns, we can trust that He will redeem our circumstances. Even if our situations and sufferings persist, we can rest in the truth that God will make all things new.

ACTION STEP

Using the space provided on the next page, journal about how you can trust God to work in your circumstances or current season.

11

LIE:

God is withholding good from me

"Even in seasons of suffering, God is working for our good."

There are moments of our lives in which God answers our prayers and gives us exactly what we have asked from Him. However, there are also moments when the opposite happens. We may have been fervently praying for God to fulfill a certain request, only to have our prayers remain seemingly unanswered. If we have been asking something from God for a long time and have not received the answer we expect, we can wonder if God is withholding from us. And, especially if what we want from God is a good thing, we can question why God will not grant us this desire. Or maybe, we are not asking for something from God, yet we feel as if our lives are made up of one negative experience after another. Perhaps other people seem to be thriving and receiving all the good things, but we are suffering and in need.

It can be discouraging to experience suffering and feel as if God is blessing everyone else but withholding from us. Yet just because it feels as if God is withholding from us does not mean He is. Psalm 84:11 tells us, "For the Lord God is a sun and shield. The Lord grants favor and honor; he does not withhold the good from those who live with integrity." We may read these words and ask, "Well, then why doesn't God give me what I desire?" Reading Psalm 84:11 along with Romans 8:28 helps provide us with further encouragement and understanding. Romans 8:28 says, "We know that all things work together for the good of those who love God, who are called according to his purpose." These verses reveal that God does not withhold good from us because God works everything for our good. This means that oftentimes, God is working in ways that differ from what we desire or expect. This is because God is a good and sovereign God, and He knows what we need far more than we do.

Psalm 84:11 and Romans 8:28 teach us how even in seasons of suffering, God is working for our good. This may be a hard truth for us to recognize or receive, but we can still choose to trust the Lord—even if we do not understand how He is working or even if we do not like the way He is working. God's sovereignty and faithfulness to work everything in our lives for good also comforts us when our prayers seemingly go unanswered. Although God may not be giving us exactly what we want, because of God's character, we know that God is giving us exactly what we need.

God withholds no good thing from those He loves but pours out good upon His people. If we still doubt this to be true, we must remember the gift of Christ. God sent us Jesus, who died on the cross for us, even though we did not deserve grace and forgiveness. But the forgiveness we receive through Christ is not the only benefit we receive. Daily, we continue to be blessed through our relationship with Jesus as we receive strength, peace, wisdom, and so much more from the Lord. Because of our relationship with Jesus, we receive good gifts every single day. In hard seasons or moments when our desires go unmet, we can remember and rest in our faithful God, who gives us exactly what we need.

───────── ACTION STEP ─────────

Spend some time in prayer, asking God to help you trust in Him and the ways He is working, even in your disappointments and unmet desires.

NO MATTER HOW BIG
OUR PAST SINS ARE,
GOD'S GRACE IS BIGGER.

LIE:

My past
disqualifies me

You just received an opportunity that is exciting and everything you hoped and prayed to receive. But then, a small voice whispers in your ear: *If they knew who you were, they wouldn't have asked you to do this.* Shame fills your heart, and immediately, you second guess the opportunity that has been presented to you.

Maybe you have not experienced this exact situation, but we can all experience moments in which the circumstances of our past lead us to believe we are disqualified from certain events or opportunities in our lives. Maybe sexual sin haunts us, and we believe we are disqualified from building a good marriage. Or perhaps crime or substance abuse clouds our past, and we think we are disqualified from being a leader. Certain sins of our past can also lead us to believe that we are disqualified from being a Christian or that we are unable to fulfill God's plan for our lives.

The enemy loves to fuel the lie that our past disqualifies us. He brings up our past experiences and circumstances to fill us with shame and make us doubt our abilities. But God's voice is different from the voice of the enemy. God does not whisper to us words of condemnation but words of grace. God knows everything about us. He knows our history and our past mistakes and still sent His Son to die for us. Our past cannot keep us from receiving the salvation God provides, nor can it keep us from fulfilling the plans and purposes He has for us. No matter how big our past sins are, God's grace is bigger.

One of the greatest testimonies of this truth comes from the Apostle Paul. Paul designates himself as "the least of the apostles, not worthy to be called an apostle" (1 Corinthians 15:9). Similarly, in 1 Timothy 1:15, Paul declares that he

"Because of Christ's grace, we can confidently step into what God has for us."

is the worst of sinners. He speaks of himself in this way because of his history of persecuting the church. But, even with Paul's terrible past, God gave him grace and appointed him as an apostle for the gospel. Paul writes in 1 Timothy 1:16, "But I received mercy for this reason, so that in me, the worst of them, Christ Jesus might demonstrate his extraordinary patience as an example to those who would believe in him for eternal life." God not only forgave Paul of his past, but God sovereignly used Paul's past as a testimony of the power of Christ's forgiveness.

Just as God forgave Paul for his past, so are we forgiven for our past in Christ. When we come to know Jesus, all of our sins are forgiven. And while the enemy can attempt to use our sins against us, God never will. Romans 8:1 tells us, "Therefore, there is now no condemnation for those in Christ Jesus." Our feelings of shame are met by the grace of Christ. Because of Christ's grace, we can confidently step into what God has for us. And like Paul, we can even use our history as a testimony to God's grace and faithfulness in our lives. When the enemy whispers that we are disqualified, we can rest in God's forgiveness. Our past does not disqualify us, for Christ's grace qualifies us.

—— ACTION STEP ——

Consider how a circumstance of your past can be used to show others the power of the gospel and God's grace.

13

LIE:

I am unworthy to be loved

While our past can make us feel disqualified, our past can also make us feel unworthy to be loved. Yet it is not just our past circumstances that can make us believe this lie but also our current circumstances. Past or current sexual sin, a situation of abuse, or a pornography addiction can make us feel ashamed. Other sin struggles we wrestle with can make us feel unlovable. How others treat us can also lead us to believe we are unworthy to be loved. Maybe a parent did not treat us with the love we should have received as a child, or perhaps someone we once had a relationship with hurt us and made us feel unlovable.

We can also feel unworthy to be loved by God. We may read of God's great love and think that other people are deserving of God's love but not us. Maybe we believe the things we have done or the things we do are too shameful for God to love us. The truth is, none of us deserve God's love. Each one of us is a sinner and can do nothing to earn God's love. Yet, even though we do not deserve God's love, God loves us still. Throughout Scripture, we see God's love in His plan to redeem and save His people. We see His love in His decision to forgive and rescue His people, even though they disobeyed Him. And we see God's love beautifully displayed in Christ. Romans 5:8 says, "But God proves his own love for us in that while we were still sinners, Christ died for us." Though we are unworthy to receive God's love, we are deemed worthy because of Christ.

If we still doubt this to be true, we must remember the power of God's love. God's love is unconditional, which means that His love is not based on what we have done, are doing, or will do. It is not influenced by our looks, skills, or successes. God's love is not determined by our actions or mistakes but by His abundant love and mercy. This gives us supreme comfort that there is nothing we can do that will prevent God from loving us. And, if we are in Christ, we can be confident that there is nothing we can do to remove God's love from us. Romans 8:38–39 says that nothing can separate us from the love of God. Not our past. Not our mistakes. Not our struggles. Nothing. The love of God that we receive through Christ is ours forever.

But then, how does the love of God impact the unworthiness we feel to be loved by others? Though there are people who may treat us as unworthy and unlovable, there are also people who will love us despite our problems and mistakes. The ability for others to love us in this way is a reflection of the gospel. Likewise, our ability to forgive and love others despite their sins reflects the beauty of the gospel and the love and forgiveness of God. Yet it is not the love of humans that determines our worth. Christ has made us worthy, and it is in Christ that we find our worth. When feelings of unworthiness arise, we can rest in the love of Christ and remember our worth in Him.

ACTION STEP

Memorize Romans 8:38–39.

14

LIE:

I do not need the Church

99

GOD USES THE BODY OF CHRIST
TO CHALLENGE, ENCOURAGE, AND
MOTIVATE US IN OUR FAITH.

14

Your alarm goes off, and you hit the snooze button with half-opened eyes. It is Sunday, and you know you need to get up for church. *It's fine for me to skip today,* you think as you roll over and fall back to sleep. Most of us have experienced moments like this or at least similar feelings. Of course, we all have times when we need to stay home from church because we are sick or cannot make it to church because we are traveling. While these instances are normal, continuously not making it to church or developing excuses for not going can lead us to believe that we do not need the Church.

But we can also believe we do not need the Church because of painful experiences we may have experienced there. Maybe people in the Church have hurt or rejected us, or certain leaders have shamed us or been unkind to us. Or perhaps we do not think we need the Church because we can live out our walk with God on our own. We think that as long as we read our Bibles and pray, we are doing what we need to do to live as a Christian. But the body of Christ is essential for every believer. Even if going to church is a struggle, or even if we have experienced past hurt from a local church, we need the Church.

In an effort to pull us into isolation, the enemy wants us to believe the lie that we do not need the Church. Community with other believers naturally allows us to voice our struggles, but isolation keeps our struggles in the dark. Without sitting under the Word and God and having others speak truth into our lives, sin can fester and grow. We need other believers who can point out sin issues in our lives, and we need the truth of God's Word to convict us and lead us to confession. While isolation may seem tempting, the Church is necessary for our spiritual well-being.

"God demonstrated His great love for us by the sacrifice of Jesus."

Hebrews 10:24–25 says, "And let us consider one another in order to provoke love and good works, not neglecting to gather together, as some are in the habit of doing, but encouraging each other, and all the more as you see the day approaching." God uses the body of Christ to challenge, encourage, and motivate us in our faith. And He uses us as members of the body to challenge, encourage, and motivate others in return. The Church is also an important part of our sanctification. When we go to church, we are shaped and sharpened by worship and the teaching of God's Word. God uses the Church to grow us in our faith and mold us into the image of Christ.

Lastly, we need the Church because the body of Christ is essential for the spreading of the gospel. As believers, we gather to hear and celebrate the gospel, but then we scatter to share the gospel. While we can share the gospel individually, the gospel spreads and the kingdom of God expands when we work together as the body to proclaim Christ. May these truths propel us to fight against complacency and isolation and remind us of the importance of the body of Christ.

ACTION STEP

Think of three believers in your life who have impacted you positively.

GOD'S WAYS ARE WHAT
LEAD US TO TRUE FREEDOM,
NOT OUR WAYS.

LIE:

I do not need God

15

Similar to the belief that we do not need the Church is the belief that we do not need God. Often, we can be tempted to believe we do not need God because of our desire for self-sufficiency. We may think that we are fully capable in our own power to make decisions and do what is right. However, we are finite beings. We have weaknesses and limitations that point out our inability to be self-sufficient. The reality of our weaknesses and limitations reveals our need for God. We were not created to operate in our own power but through the power of the Lord.

As humans, we possess not only weaknesses and limits but also sinful hearts. Jeremiah 17:9 tells us, "The heart is more deceitful than anything else, and incurable—who can understand it?" We may think our hearts and minds can guide us in the right way to go, but because we are sinful, we will lead ourselves astray. No matter how wise we try to be, we will still make mistakes and stumble into sin.

Our limits and sins point to the fact that we are not meant to live as self-relying and self-sustaining humans. Each one of us was created to worship and glorify God, follow Him, and depend on Him. When we decide that we are the main source of authority in our lives and God is not, we sink deeper into sin.

Jeremiah 17:9 reminds us of how deeply sinful our hearts are. Our sin and disobedience deserve punishment because we have sinned against a holy and righteous God. However, there is nothing we can do in our own power to save ourselves from this punishment. Even if we try to be a "good" person, our moral choices and good deeds do nothing to release us from the punishment we deserve. Romans 3:10 and 3:23 tell us how there is no one righteous, and we all sin

"We were not created to operate in our own power but through the power of the Lord."

and fall short of the glory of God. But this is why we need God, for only God has the power to save us from our sin.

In His kindness, God sent us Jesus to bring us salvation. Through His death and resurrection, Christ gives us grace that cleanses our sinful and prideful hearts. When we come to faith in Christ, we receive His strength and power to help us walk in obedience to God. God's ways are what lead us to true freedom, not our ways. When we depend on God, submit to His ways, and choose to follow Him, we will make choices that honor and glorify Him. We will live as the holy people He created us to be, and we will experience the freedom that comes from serving Him.

Our fickle hearts may tell us that we do not need God, but we are lost without Him. Instead of ignoring our weaknesses, limitations, and sins, let us recognize our utter dependence on the Lord. As we daily admit our need for God and place our dependence on Him, we will rest in His strength, wisdom, and righteousness that help us truly live.

ACTION STEP

List several ways you need to rely on God in your life.

16

LIE:

I need the perfect house, car, family, etc. to be happy

When we turn on the television, we often see commercials trying to sell us something. For example, you might see a group of people laughing and holding the same drink, or maybe you see someone driving a car and receiving the attention of an attractive person nearby. These commercials are not just trying to sell us a product but a story or message. Viewing these scenes can lead us to think that we need that drink to be popular and have lots of friends or that we need that car to be appealing to the opposite sex.

Commercials and advertisements proclaim the lie that we need certain products to be happy, but social media can also fuel this lie. We can see images of what appears to be a perfect home or family and think we need what they have to feel happy, satisfied, and affirmed. But the narrative that social media and advertisements often seek to tell always fails to fulfill us. We may buy that one product or obtain that perfect house, only to find ourselves still dissatisfied. This dissatisfaction we and so many others feel is meant to point to the fact that our satisfaction is not found in the things of this world. Our satisfaction is found in Christ alone.

One of the reasons we can forget this truth is because we settle for quick doses of contentment and joy. We make a purchase or receive something we desire, and we experience that instant feeling of gratification. But quick doses of satisfaction do not provide lasting contentment. We might think we are satisfied, but just as hunger pains come again after a meal, so does the feeling of emptiness return. While many choose to ignore this reality and keep going to temporary sources for satisfaction, we do not have to operate this way as followers of Christ. As believers, we have all we need in Jesus. This is why Paul says in Philippians 4:12–13, "In any and all circumstances I have learned the secret of being content—whether well fed or hungry, whether in abundance or in need. I am able to do all things through him who strengthens me."

Even though Paul experienced seasons of abundance and need, he knew that he could be content in either circumstance because of his relationship with Christ and his contentment in Him. When we place our contentment in Christ, our joy will not rise or fall depending on our circumstances or needs. In Christ, our contentment and joy remain secure. And because we are placing our contentment in an eternal God, our satisfaction in Christ is long-lasting. We no longer need to settle for temporary morsels when we are feasting on the Bread of Life.

However, our flesh will cause us to still desire the things of this world to feel happy and satisfied. In the moments we find ourselves tempted by temporary pleasures, let us remember the supremacy of Christ. Our salvation in Christ and our relationship with Him make us truly satisfied. May we turn away from what the world proclaims is necessary to rest in the One who is our greatest necessity. In Christ, we find true joy and lasting satisfaction.

ACTION STEP

Consider one or two items you are currently clinging to for satisfaction. Come up with one practical way to lessen your hold on this thing or things so that your satisfaction might instead be rooted in Christ.

17

LIE:

I do not have enough time

AS BELIEVERS, WE USE OUR TIME TO GIVE GOD GLORY.

Our days never seem to be long enough. Even if we succeed in doing everything on our to-do lists, there is always something else that needs to be done. We simply can't do all we desire with the time we are given. This reality can cause us to make excuses. For example, there might be something important we know we need to do but instead, we shrug it off because we say there is not enough time. And, while there are certainly circumstances and seasons that hinder our abilities, we must remember: God has given us the time to do what is important.

Often, we say that we do not have enough time because we want to avoid doing what is hard or requires effort. One of the ways we can do this is in our Bible study. We can look at our schedules and say to ourselves, There isn't any time for me to read my Bible today. But then we find time to scroll on our phones or watch television. We can also procrastinate in other ways, like putting off sharing the gospel with a family member or taking our car in for a tune-up. Yet, if that family member passes or our car breaks down, we can regret that we did not use the available time more intentionally before it was too late.

Our failure to use our time intentionally and wisely is not meant to move us to despair but action. Because of Christ, we receive forgiveness for our excuses and missed opportunities. But the grace and forgiveness of Christ should motivate us to use our time wisely. As believers, we use our time to give God glory. When we become consumed with our desires alone and what makes us comfortable, we will use our time to please ourselves rather than the Lord. But, when we remember what Christ has done to give us life, we will take up the life that we have received with the desire to serve and glorify the Lord.

"God gives us time, but He also gives us rest."

Moses prays in Psalm 90:12, "Teach us to number our days carefully so that we may develop wisdom in our hearts." His words teach us how we live with wisdom when we acknowledge the importance—and the fleeting nature—of time. Moses's prayer also reminds us how we can ask God to help us use our time wisely. We can ask the Lord to help us live with a sense of urgency in the present and not neglect the time He has graciously provided. And, in the moments we fail, we can rest in the grace of Christ and the power of the Spirit that helps us endure.

However, while we should be mindful of using our time wisely, we should also remember the importance of rest. God gives us time, but He also gives us rest. We have limits as humans, and while God helps us accomplish what is important, we should not place expectations on ourselves to do everything. We should be careful not to overwhelm ourselves with doing as much as possible while neglecting the rest our bodies need. As we seek to use our time to give God glory and enjoy the gift of rest, we will live faithfully unto the Lord.

ACTION STEP

Think of one area in your life in which you are not using your time wisely, and come up with one practical way you can use that time for something better and wiser.

IN HIS SOVEREIGNTY
AND PROVIDENCE,
GOD ORCHESTRATES
EVENTS ACCORDING TO
HIS PERFECT WILL.

18

LIE:

I messed up God's
plan for me

Discerning the right decision to make can be a frustrating and overwhelming task. We might think we are doing what God has called us to do, only to then feel as if we made a mistake. Perhaps the job we decided to take is not what we expected, and we feel stuck in a place we do not want to be. Or maybe we decided to switch majors but then find it difficult to find work. In these moments, we can feel as if we have messed up God's plan because of our choices.

But we can also feel as if we have messed up God's plans when we make sinful choices. Maybe an unplanned pregnancy results from our decision to have sex outside of marriage. Or perhaps substance abuse plagues our lives, and we feel stuck in a cycle of unhealthy habits. These decisions might make us feel ashamed and afraid that our lives have ruined God's plans and purposes.

While sinful choices can complicate our lives and inhibit certain opportunities, nothing can ruin God's plans. One of the most comforting truths about God is that He is sovereign. In His sovereignty and providence, God orchestrates events according to His perfect will. This means that whatever God has ordained to happen will always come to pass. While God's sovereignty can be hard to grasp, the fact that God's plans will always succeed is incredibly encouraging. Because of God's sovereignty, we do not have to ever worry that we have messed up God's plans. After all, to believe this lie is to believe that we have more power than the God of the universe. Thankfully, we do not have enough power to ruin God's plans, and that is a reason to rejoice.

Another aspect of God's sovereignty is that He works through our sinful choices and mistakes. Even if we do something that is not pleasing to the Lord, we can be con-

"As we seek to glorify God in our decisions, we can trust He will guide us in His way."

fident that He will still work through our situation to accomplish His purposes. If we doubt this to be true, we can remind ourselves of the story of the Israelites, God's chosen people. He formed a covenant with them and promised to lead, guide, and form them into a thriving nation. But Israel did not listen to God's commands, and they soon turned away from Him to worship false gods. All throughout the Old Testament, we see how Israel failed to uphold their end of their covenant with God and did not walk in His ways. Their disobedience and unrepentance ultimately led them to be ripped away from their land and placed into exile. But, even though Israel failed in their obedience to God, God was faithful to fulfill His covenant and His plan of redemption for His people. And ultimately, we know this to be true because of Christ.

Just as Israel's unfaithfulness could not thwart God's plans, our choices and failures cannot thwart God's plans. Yet this truth is not a license to do whatever we please but should encourage us to keep seeking after faithfulness to the Lord. As we seek to glorify God in our decisions, we can trust He will guide us in His way.

ACTION STEP

Meditate on Jeremiah 29:11 and Psalm 33:11, and ask the Lord to help you trust His plans and walk in His ways.

19

LIE:

My feelings and emotions control and define me

You lash out at your kids for the third time today. You wake up in the morning with a cloud over your head that will not disappear. You feel the rush of overwhelming fear as you get behind the wheel of your car. Anger, sadness, and fear are but several of many other emotions and feelings we experience. For some of us, these feelings and emotions come and go, but for others, they are part of our everyday lives.

When we describe our emotions or feelings, we often say, "I'm angry," or "I'm sad." But when certain emotions or feelings regularly occur, we may begin to believe that they control, own, and define us. This belief can cause our feelings and emotions to be not just something we experience but rather a part of who we are — our identity. Even though emotions and feelings like anger, sadness, and fear are frustrating and discouraging, we do not have to believe the lie that they define us. Who we are in Christ defines us most of all.

It is important to remember that God has gifted us with emotions and feelings. Our emotions and feelings are meant to reveal what is in our hearts. Often, but not always, anger may be a sign that we need to work on patience and forgiveness with others. And even though sadness or fear may point us to a hormonal imbalance, these feelings may also reveal a misplaced trust in the Lord. When we fail to do the hard but necessary task of examining our emotions, our feelings, and their root cause, it can become easy to succumb to our emotions and feelings. Instead of understanding and evaluating how we can train our emotions and what the correct response to our feelings should be, we can lean on the excuse that how we feel and act is just a part of who we are.

But, when we remember that who we are in Christ defines us, we can look at our emotions and feelings through the lens of the gospel. In doing so, we see how, because of our relationship with Christ, it is Jesus who owns us, not our emotions and feelings. And, because Christ set us free from the power of sin, we also see how our emotions and feelings do not ultimately control us. We might not be able to control when certain emotions and feelings arise, but we can control our response to them. The Holy Spirit helps us fight against sinful responses to our feelings and gives us the strength to react in godly ways to our emotions. And, even if fighting anxiety or depression is a life-long battle, we can remember that this battle will not last forever. When Christ returns, He will deliver us from all that plagues us in the present, and we will live in eternal peace.

Until this day, we can continue with God's help to navigate our emotions and feelings with wisdom. We can rest in His strength when fighting anger is difficult, and we can rest in His peace when fear arises. And when the enemy tries to make us believe that our emotions and feelings define us, we can rest in the truth that we are not our anger, anxiety, or depression—we are the Lord's.

ACTION STEP

Look up the passage listed with each emotion on the next page, and then list how you can apply the truth from Scripture when you experience that emotion.

EMOTION	SCRIPTURE	APPLICATION
Fear	PSALM 56:3-4	
Anger	JAMES 1:19-20	
Jealousy	JAMES 3:14-17	
Joy	ROMANS 15:13	
Resentment	EPHESIANS 4:31-32	
Sadness	PSALM 34:17-18	

20

LIE:

I am unforgivable

"

OUR GOD IS SLOW TO ANGER AND
ABOUNDING IN FAITHFUL LOVE,
FORGIVING INIQUITY AND REBELLION.

You did it again. The sin that you promised you would never repeat. That bad habit that you have prayed so hard to quit. Shame overwhelms you, and tears fill your eyes. *God can't possibly forgive me*, you think to yourself.

Our struggle to obey God can be discouraging. And, if our view of the Lord is skewed, we can believe that God is holding up a chalkboard, waiting to draw strike three and declare us out of His grace. But that is not the God we serve. Our God is slow to anger and abounding in faithful love, forgiving iniquity and rebellion (Numbers 14:18). To declare these truths further, God sent us Jesus, whose blood covers our iniquities and whose grace deems us forgiven. If we are in Christ, we can have full confidence that the forgiveness we receive through Jesus is ours forever. Even on our worst days, God's grace remains.

This means that if we are in Christ, there is nothing we have done or will do that will remove God's grace from us. Because of Christ, we are fully and eternally forgiven. As the Apostle John proclaims in 1 John 1:9, "If we confess our sins, he is faithful and righteous to forgive us our sins and to cleanse us from all unrighteousness." This should bring us incredible comfort when we falter in our faithfulness to the Lord. As believers, we have complete assurance that God forgives our every sin—past, present, and future.

But maybe some of us still feel as if what we have done is truly unforgivable. Perhaps we have done something that others would view as the worst possible sin. Throughout the Gospels, we receive example after example of sinful people who encountered the grace of Christ. During Jesus's time on earth, He forgave women caught up in sexual sin (John 8:10–11), reviled tax collectors (Luke 19:1–10), and His disciples who abandoned Him (John 21:15–19). Even as Jesus hung on the cross, He forgave the thief next to Him and prayed for God's mercy to be upon those who mocked Him (Luke 23:34, 39–43). Christ's forgiveness in the Gospels demonstrates how there is no one too sinful to receive Christ's grace. Jesus invites all sinners to come to Him and be forgiven. Even what seems unforgivable to us remains forgivable in Christ.

And because Christ's grace was not given to us based on what we have done but based on what Christ has done, we can be confident that Christ's grace remains overflowing forever. The cross of Christ and the blood of Jesus stand as a reminder of Christ's permanent forgiveness. Therefore, in the moments when the enemy whispers to us that we are unforgivable, we can look to the cross and listen to the voice of our Savior that says we are forgiven. We can freely confess our sins and continue to seek holiness as we rest in God's forgiveness. Because of Jesus, we are declared innocent in the eyes of God, no matter the sin that taints our hearts or plagues our past. For even the dirtiest stains of sin have been washed clean by Jesus's grace.

--- ACTION STEP ---

Spend some time in prayer, thanking God for His forgiveness and asking that He will help you to regularly remember and rest in His grace.

THE LOVE OF OUR FATHER
REMAINS STRONG AND STEADY,
EVEN WHEN WE ARE WILLFUL
AND WAYWARD.

LIE:

I cannot come back to God if I have turned away from Him

21

Luke 15 tells the story of the prodigal son. In this parable, a young man demands his inheritance from his father and leaves home to pursue his own desires. But after he has squandered his money, he realizes that he has led himself to ruin. So the son chooses to come back home, hoping his father will at least make him one of his servants. As he nears home, his father sees him from a distance, runs to him, and kisses him. The son says to his father, "Father, I have sinned against heaven and in your sight. I'm no longer worthy to be called your son" (Luke 15:21). But his father clothes him and throws a celebration in honor of his son's return.

Those of us who have turned away from God to go our own way are like the prodigal son in this passage. But our journeys as the prodigal son may look different depending on our situations. For example, perhaps we grew up going to church and followed God for a while, only to let our doubts take over and cause us to stop following Him. It may have been years since we can remember praying to the Lord or seeking obedience to Him. Or, for some of us, maybe it hasn't been years but a few weeks or perhaps even a few minutes. Because of our sinful nature, we continually fail to remain obedient and faithful to the Lord. We go our own way more than we realize, and the longer we go our own way, the easier it can be to become ashamed of our waywardness. We may think we are too far gone to return to the Lord. But, whether we have completely turned from Him or struggle to remain faithful to Him, we do not have to believe the lie that we cannot come back to God.

The good news is that we serve a God who is just like the father in the parable of the prodigal son. God will always welcome us back to Him, no matter how far we have strayed. This is true because of Jesus. As sinners, there is nothing

"God is always waiting with open arms for us to come back to Him."

we can do on our own to earn God's favor and remain a permanent part of His family. But this is why Jesus came and died on the cross for us. Through His death and resurrection, Jesus made it possible for our sins to be forgiven and for us to be permanently reconciled with our heavenly Father. Because of Christ, we belong to God and His family forever. The love of our Father remains strong and steady, even when we are willful and wayward. For those of us in Christ, we can be confident that God always sees us as His beloved sons and daughters, even if we once turned from Him to go our own way.

God is always waiting with open arms for us to come back to Him. And, even in the moments we stray, we do not have to be ashamed of our waywardness because of our relationship with Jesus. Instead, we can acknowledge and repent from our unfaithfulness and rest in the grace of our heavenly Father. If we are in Christ, we cannot outrun the grace of our God. He will always pursue us and welcome us home.

ACTION STEP

Spend some time in prayer, confessing to God how you have strayed from Him and asking for His help to rest in His grace and remain close to Him.

22

LIE:

Having a child makes me whole

Children are a sweet gift. While they require a lot of work and can cause many sleepless nights and moments of frustration, they bring us joy. It is a gift to be a parent, for parents have a special role in teaching and raising up young minds. However, it is possible to believe that we need a child to make us whole. Sadly, many people have perpetuated this lie, even people within the Church. People have praised parenthood so much that they can cause themselves and others to believe that parenthood is the pinnacle achievement of womanhood. These beliefs can cause those who are single, struggling with infertility, or not at a place to have children yet to feel like a part of them is missing—that the only way to be complete is to have a child.

While having a child is special and evidence of God's grace, what we ultimately need is not a child but Jesus. It is not children who make us whole; it is Christ. Only Jesus can fill the ache within our hearts and give us lasting satisfaction. When we establish parenthood as the highest goal for women, the truth that Jesus is all that we need becomes skewed. This can cause us and others to believe that Jesus plus parenthood gives us completion. But this is not what God's Word says. Scripture tells us that Christ's grace is the only thing we need for true joy, life, and salvation.

Establishing parenthood as the highest goal can also cause us to skew the purpose for which we were created. Genesis 1:28 tells us that God commanded Adam and Eve to "be fruitful, multiply, fill the earth, and subdue it." This command involves Adam and Eve bearing children so that they

can fill the earth with people who will love and worship God.
Some may point to this command and say this states our
purpose as humans. Others may say this command applies
to all people today, and to disobey it is not to live as God
commands. While we see children and parenthood held in
high regard in the Bible, God's Word does not say that parenthood is our ultimate purpose. Instead, we see throughout
Scripture that God's people are to worship God and make
His name known (Psalm 105:1, Matthew 22:36–38). This is
the purpose for which God created us.

Through Jesus, we can fulfill our purpose, and as we worship God and are obedient to Him, we will walk as the
people He created us to be. For some of us, God will bless
us with parenthood as a way to worship Him and make
His name known, but this does not mean parenthood is
the only way to do so. While God can use parenthood to
glorify Him, we can glorify the Lord regardless of whether
we are a parent. All believers can be faithful followers of
Christ and workers for God's kingdom, no matter their
season or sphere of influence. Therefore, in the moments
we feel like we are incomplete because we lack children,
let us remember our greatest need and true purpose — to
know Jesus and live for Him.

ACTION STEP

*Consider how God is using your specific season of
life — whether you are single, married without kids,
married with kids, a single parent, or widowed — for
your good and His glory.*

23

LIE:

Everyone has it all together but me

" "

OUR INABILITY TO HAVE IT ALL
TOGETHER PROPELS US TO REST
IN THE ONE WHO DOES.

"We may shame ourselves for how we fall short, but Christ died for us, fully knowing our shortcomings."

It is Monday morning, and you open your eyes from sleep. Confused at why it seems brighter than normal, you glance at the clock and realize you forgot to set your alarm. It is 9:30, which means your kids are very late for school. You do your best to get them dressed and in the car, all the while trying to run a comb through your own hair. As you rush your kids into school, you pass another mother who is leaving. Her hair is neat, her makeup is flawless, and her clothes are pristine. As you wrap your coat around your pajamas, you duck your head to avoid her gaze, ashamed at your disorder compared to her order.

Whether you can relate to this example or not, we can all relate to experiencing moments of failure or frazzle that lead us to believe everyone has it all together—except us. We can feel as if everyone lives neatly ordered lives while we are scrambling around trying to pick up the pieces of our own. And, while these hectic moments may point out changes we need to make in our lives, the belief that we are the only ones who struggle with this is untrue. Each one of us falls short of perfection because we are not God. Only God is perfect and the One who truly has it "all together." Because we are human and sinful, we make mistakes and have weaknesses. We also live in a broken world, which means that each of us experiences struggles and suffering. Someone may look like they have it all together on the outside, but inside, they may be wrestling with insecurity or struggling with shame. Even the mother in the preceding scenario could have been walking through a hidden, painful situation. We all struggle in one way or another, and our brokenness keeps us from having it all together.

But the good news is, because of Jesus, we are loved even though we are weak and broken. We may shame ourselves for how we fall short, but Christ died for us, fully knowing our shortcomings. And because of His death on the cross, we receive grace for our brokenness. When we rest in Christ's grace, we will not berate ourselves for how we fall short. Instead, we will rely on His strength to keep pursuing faithfulness to God despite our limitations and weaknesses. Rather than comparing ourselves to others, we can focus on how God is growing and teaching us, even in the messiness of life. And we can rely on His Spirit to help us pursue and mature in Christlikeness.

The truth that no one has it all together should also motivate us to love and serve others. We are not always aware of people's struggles, which means we should actively seek ways we can care for and help one another. Instead of comparing ourselves to others, we can consider how we can come alongside them to shoulder their burdens and weaknesses. And, because people do not always know our struggles, we should allow ourselves to be vulnerable with others and ask for their help.

Each one of us struggles and is broken, but we are not left without aid. Our inability to have it all together propels us to rest in the One who does.

ACTION STEP

Think of one person you can intentionally come alongside to help and encourage, and make a plan to do so this week.

WHILE GOD GRACIOUSLY
ALLOWS US TO MAKE CHOICES,
HE IS THE ONE WHO IS
ULTIMATELY IN CONTROL.

24

LIE:

I am in control
of my life

The poet William Ernest Henley once wrote, "I am the master of my fate, I am the captain of my soul." This quote and others with the same message promote the idea that humans have individual autonomy—that we are the ones who set the course of our paths and the ones who are ultimately in control. And, because of sin, we operate this way more often than we might realize. Our sinful flesh desires to be in charge. We like to be the ones who take the steering wheel instead of releasing it into God's hands. This is why it can be a struggle to obey God's commands, even if we are followers of Jesus. We can experience the tension between desiring to do what God says and doing what we want. But, while God graciously allows us to make choices, He is the One who is ultimately in control.

God's sovereignty is connected to the truth that He is ultimately in control. God sovereignly controls the world and the events that take place within our world. This does not mean that God always causes something to happen, but in His divine sovereignty, He works through everything to accomplish His purposes. However, God also graciously grants humans free will. He allows us to make choices and plans, and because we are given free will, we are the ones who are held responsible for the choices we make and the consequences of those actions. But thankfully, God is the One who works through our decisions and plans. His purposes will always come to fruition no matter our choices and actions. As Proverbs 19:21 tells us, "Many plans are in a person's heart, but the Lord's decree will prevail."

The truth that God is the One who is ultimately in control is meant to humble us and motivate us to yield to God's sovereignty. The gift of free will is not a license to do what we please with no thought to the consequences of our actions.

"Trusting in God's plans and obeying His ways is what leads to true freedom."

It does not give us permission to ignore God's ultimate authority and seek to be the ones in power. Unfortunately, this is what happened when sin entered the world. It was Adam and Eve's choice to ignore God's commands and resist obedience to His ultimate authority. Thankfully, because God is good and sovereign, He worked through the folly of Adam and Eve to put forth a plan of redemption. He saved us from the error of our ways by sending us Jesus. But, when we come to faith in Christ, we are to submit to Him completely. We are to deny ourselves and take up our cross to follow Jesus (Mark 8:34).

The life of faith and discipleship is a life of releasing our control to trust in God's ultimate control. It involves laying down our own will so that we can submit to God's will. While we may be tempted to believe that placing control in our own hands leads to true freedom, trusting in God's plans and obeying His ways is what leads to true freedom. Therefore, let us surrender our grip on our lives and submit to the God who holds our lives in His hands.

— ACTION STEP —

Consider one area of your life in which you are currently struggling to give God control. Spend some time in prayer, asking God to help you surrender control and trust Him in this area.

25

LIE:

I cannot do what God has called me to do

Have you ever received a job offer or new opportunity that made you nervous? Or has God ever led you to do something you felt completely unprepared to do? When these moments arise, it can be easy to question why God chose us and believe we are ill-equipped for the task ahead. Doubting God's calling for our lives or feeling insecure about what He has brought us to can make us afraid to move forward. We might ask ourselves, *What if I fail?* Or we might think to ourselves, *Someone else is probably more fit to do this than me. I am incapable.* What God has led us to do can certainly feel like a daunting task, but we do not have to believe that we cannot succeed in what God has called us to do. What God calls us to, He will equip us to accomplish.

One of the greatest biblical examples of this truth is the story of Moses. When God called Moses to be the one who would lead the Israelites out of slavery, Moses was apprehensive about this call. In fact, he even tried to tell God that he chose the wrong man for the job. Moses told God, "Please, Lord, I have never been eloquent—either in the past or recently or since you have been speaking to your servant—because my mouth and my tongue are sluggish" (Exodus 4:10). But even when God promised how He would be with Moses and help him speak, Moses still asked for God to send someone else. Although God allowed Moses's brother, Aaron, to help Moses speak, God still used Moses—weaknesses and insecurities and all—to deliver His people.

Moses is one of many examples in Scripture of seemingly ill-equipped people used by God. Their examples teach us how no task or role is too great for us to do with God's help. On our own, we are certainly helpless and weak, but the wonderful truth about being a believer is that we are never on our own. God's power within us helps us accomplish what He has for us. And, because it is the Lord who causes us to succeed in what He calls us to do, we can step forward in confidence. As God tells us in Isaiah 41:10, "Do not fear, for I am with you; do not be afraid, for I am your God. I will strengthen you; I will help you; I will hold on to you with my righteous right hand."

God is the One who empowers us to succeed in every good work (2 Corinthians 9:8–9). His power works through our weaknesses to accomplish His good purposes. Therefore, the moments we feel ill-equipped are the moments we witness God's power displayed. When we allow ourselves to become fixated on our insecurities, we can miss the ways that God is working within us. So let us not be afraid of what God calls us to do. Let us not shrink back but step forward in faith. Without God, we are ill-equipped, but because of God's presence and power with us and within us, we are fully equipped for whatever He calls us to do.

ACTION STEP

Think of a time in your life when you witnessed God help you do something you thought you could not do.

26

LIE:

I am alone

> BECAUSE OF CHRIST'S GRACE, WE ARE
> BOUND TOGETHER IN A UNION WITH
> GOD THAT CAN NEVER BREAK.

You have nobody. No one cares about you. You are alone. These thoughts can often enter our minds when someone rejects, alienates, or abandons us. Maybe someone you care about turned their back on you, maybe you sit alone on Sunday mornings, or maybe your spouse spends more time away from you than with you. Or perhaps you think these thoughts because you know people are hanging out without you while you are home by yourself on another Friday night. Believing that we are alone can lead us to feel as if no one truly loves or cares for us, or we can begin to worry that the people we do know and love will eventually leave us. Feeling lonely can also cause us to turn inward and wonder what is wrong with us that has caused us to be so alone.

Combating loneliness can be a struggle. Even if we are in a crowded room, we can still feel as if we are all alone. Often, we feel alone because we are not receiving the companionship we desire or the relationship we crave. Perhaps you think that if only you had more friends or if only you were married, then you would not feel so alone. However, our feelings of loneliness are ultimately not meant to be resolved through others but through our relationship with God.

God created us for Himself, but sin separates us from Him. Yet God made a way for us to be reunited with Him once again by sending us Jesus. When we come to faith in Christ, we are reconciled, or made right, in our relationship with God once again. Because of Christ's grace, we are bound together in a union with God that can never break. He is ours, and we are His forever. If we are in Christ, we are never alone. We have the presence of God with us always, no matter where we go or what we

"We are never alone because God is with us."

do. Unlike our human relationships, we can have complete assurance that God will never leave us. As Matthew 28:20 says, "I am with you always, to the end of the age."

However, because God is an invisible God, we might feel as if we need the physical presence of others to make us feel less alone. But we can still be aware of God's presence, even if we cannot physically feel Him. We can experience God's presence when we pray or open up His Word. We can also experience God's presence more powerfully when we gather with other brothers and sisters in Christ. In fact, one of the ways we can combat loneliness is by remembering that we belong to an eternal family.

The Christian life is not an isolated life, for we are part of the family of God. One day, we will experience what it is like to live with this family forever, but we receive a foretaste of that reality in the present. When we go to church or fellowship with other believers, we are reminded how we are not alone. In His kindness, God uses the physical presence of other believers to remind us of His loving presence with us. But, even on the days when we are apart from others, we are never alone because God is with us.

—————————— ACTION STEP ——————————

Think of a couple of people God has placed in your life, and thank God for these people.

WE HAVE A GOD WHO
COMFORTS US IN OUR PAIN
AND HAS THE POWER TO
HEAL OUR EVERY WOUND.

LIE:

I cannot heal from my past or current pain

You lie on your bed with tears streaming down your face. Your heart feels broken, and your body is overcome with grief. *Will I feel like this forever?* You think to yourself. It appears this way at the moment—like your shattered heart will never repair. The pain feels too real and too heavy to ever lift.

When we experience heartbreak or grief, it can certainly seem like we will never heal. Perhaps a family member did something that hurt you, a loved one passed away, or your best friend turned their back on you. But while heartbreak and grief are hard, we do not have to feel as if our wounds will remain. We have a God who comforts us in our pain and has the power to heal our every wound.

Reading His Word is one way we can be reminded of how He comforts us. Psalm 34:18 tells us, "The Lord is near the brokenhearted; he saves those crushed in spirit." In our moments of grief and despair, God is with us. He is near to us in our pain, and His presence resides with us in our pain. This verse promises not only God's nearness but also His salvation. Because our God is a God of salvation, we can be confident that He will bring us out of our suffering, even if it takes time. Second Corinthians 1:3–4 also says, "Blessed be the God and Father of our Lord Jesus Christ, the Father of mercies and the God of all comfort. He comforts us in all our affliction ..." God comforts our broken hearts. He is the God of all comfort, which means that His comfort is better than anything this world can supply. We might believe that this pain is too great for God's comfort, but God comforts us in all of our afflictions, no matter how great they may seem.

Ultimately, we can be confident that God will heal our wounds because He has done so in Christ. Through the sac-

"God comforts us in all of our afflictions, no matter how great they may seem."

rifice of Christ, we receive salvation that heals the wounds of our sin and shame. His grace heals our broken hearts and makes them whole in Him. And, if Christ has healed our greatest wound, He can surely heal our lesser wounds.

Yet this healing may take time. Some of us who experience a great loss may find that God's healing will be a slow process over a long period of time, while others may find that this healing takes place faster than originally thought. However, while we wait for healing, our greatest comfort is the truth that Christ will make all things new. This pain that we are feeling will not last forever because, one day, Christ will remove all pain for eternity. Even if ultimate healing does not occur in this life, we can be confident that it will happen in the next.

But for now, as we experience our grief and pain, we can lean into the God of comfort. We can rest in His peace and strength to help us move forward, even in our brokenness. We can even rejoice, knowing that God will bring us out of this grief, and we can trust in Him until that time comes. There is no hurt, no loss, and no rejection for which God cannot and will not provide healing.

ACTION STEP

Ask a friend or trusted believer to share how they have seen God bring healing from a past hurt in their own lives.

28

LIE:

I need to do what is best for me

Has anyone ever told you before, "You just need to do what is best for you"? These words are often read in self-help books and spoken between characters on television shows as a means to encourage them to focus on their own needs. On the surface, this idea seems good. And in one way, we should think about what we need. We should take care of ourselves and be mindful of what our bodies and minds need to be healthy. If we are put into situations of harm, we should think about what is best for us, which would be to remove ourselves and be safe. But too often, this idea promotes a self-centered attitude. The choice to do what is best for us can cause us to excuse sin in our lives and hurt others. However, Scripture speaks a different narrative than this popular lie. God's Word instructs us to not focus primarily on ourselves but on others.

Philippians 2:3–4 says, "Do nothing out of selfish ambition or conceit, but in humility consider others as more important than yourselves. Everyone should look not to his own interests, but rather to the interests of others." These verses do not say that we should ignore our own interests. Instead, these verses teach that we should think of others more than ourselves. Instead of being consumed with ourselves, we are to humbly think of others and treat others as more important. It can be hard to act this way, not only because we live in a rather self-centered world but also because we have sinful flesh. Our flesh naturally desires to do what we want and what will make us the happiest. But God created us to care about others. This is why many of the Ten Commandments are centered on the right treatment of others and why God commanded us to love our neighbor as ourselves (Leviticus 19:18). And these are not simply Old Testament commands. Jesus Himself echoes the words of the Old Testament as He teaches how the second greatest commandment is to love your neighbor as yourself (Mark 12:31).

As we care for and love others, we reflect our God, who loves and cares for us. Jesus demonstrated this love for us on the cross. In fact, Paul's words in Philippians 2:3–4 are followed by Jesus's example of sacrificial love. Paul tells us how Jesus willingly chose to leave His glorious position on high to become a humble servant. Jesus could have done what was "best" for Him by boasting in His glory and avoiding the cross, but He did not. Instead, He did what was best for us: laying Himself down on the cross so we could be forgiven. Jesus is the perfect example of humility and sacrificial service for others. As believers, we are to imitate the example of Jesus by putting others' needs before our own and making sacrifices to love and care for others.

In the moments when this feels hard, we are to remind ourselves of what Jesus did for us. Christ's work on the cross motivates our humility and propels us to lay down our pride. As we walk in humility, we emulate our Savior who humbled Himself for our sake.

ACTION STEP

List three ways you can practically put others before yourself this week.

29

LIE:

What I have to say does not matter

99

GOD HAS GIVEN US EACH A VOICE
TO ENCOURAGE, GUIDE,
AND SPEAK TRUTH.

29

God is a God who speaks. The first few words of Scripture reveal how God used His voice to cause light to burst forth and order creation. Since we are made in the image of God, our voices matter. We reflect the God who speaks life in and through our own words. This means that each and every person's voice matters. Even if others speak more eloquently than us, our words and what we desire to say carry weight.

It can be easy, especially for those of us who are more naturally introverted, to feel that it is those who are more extroverted or talented in speaking whose voices matter most. But when we turn to the pages of Scripture, we see how the command to use our voices and use them wisely is a command for all people. For example, Proverbs 31:8 exhorts us to "speak up for those who have no voice," and Zechariah 8:16 says, "These are the things you must do: Speak truth to one another…"

God has given us each a voice to encourage, guide, and speak truth. And because God has created and gifted each one of us uniquely, He intentionally uses our experiences and personalities to speak words that impact others. We may believe that our voice does not matter, but there are people who need to hear what we have to say. What we have to say also matters because each believer is called to share the gospel. By the power of the Spirit, God uses our words to speak the wondrous truths of the gospel, impacting others with this truth and changing hearts. If we simply let the more "eloquent" ones handle the proclaiming of the gospel, we would miss out on important opportunities to share the good news of Jesus Christ.

If "death and life are in the power of the tongue" (Proverbs 18:21), then what we say and how we say it certainly

"Even if our voice shakes, we can lean on the power of the Spirit to speak words of life."

matter. Therefore, we should use our voices wisely as believers and aim to speak graciously. When we feel afraid or ill-equipped to speak up, we can remember that it is through the power of the Holy Spirit that we can use our voices for good. The Spirit motivates, empowers, and enables us to speak God-honoring words. An example of this is found in Luke 12:11–12, in which Jesus says, "Whenever they bring you before synagogues and rulers and authorities, don't worry about how you should defend yourselves or what you should say. For the Holy Spirit will teach you at that very hour what must be said." Even if our voice shakes, we can lean on the power of the Spirit to speak words of life.

As we remember the Spirit within us and rely on His power, we will be motivated to speak up and use our voices. We will understand the impact that our words of encouragement and truth can bring in people's lives and how our sharing of the gospel can change hearts. As we remind ourselves that we are made in the image of God, we will be encouraged to reflect our God who speaks.

--- ACTION STEP ---

Consider a time when God used something you said to help and encourage another.

INSTEAD OF DESIRING TO
BE LIKE OTHERS, OUR
GREATEST DESIRE SHOULD
BE TO BE LIKE JESUS.

LIE:

I would be happy,
if only I were more
like _____

We can scroll on our phones and become envious of someone who has more followers than us. We can look around at church and wish we could be like the woman who has more friends than us. The unhealthy habit of comparison can enable us to look at those who seem happy and thriving and feel like we need to be more like them. We may examine ourselves and believe that we must change to experience the happiness or successes of others. Comparison can lie to us and cause us to make assumptions that are not always true.

We might think the girl on social media with the many followers has a great life, but we do not see the struggles that are not displayed online. We may assume that the woman with lots of friends feels affirmed and well-liked, but we do not see the inward insecurities she battles. Comparison can also lie to us by leading us to believe that becoming more like others will promise happiness. And, while we can learn from others and make wise and healthy changes in our lives, changing ourselves to be like other people does not promise joy. In fact, it can lead to even further discouragement when we realize we still do not have what we desire, even after changing ourselves.

The desire to be like others causes us to devalue the person God created us to be. God has made each one of us intentionally, and who He has created us to be is not to be changed but celebrated. And, while God desires for each one of us to develop in Christlikeness and walk in holiness, He does not want us to change the unique ways we have been designed. Our physical appearances, personalities, and skills were given to us by a good and intentional God. When we embrace these gifts and use them in God-glorifying ways, we will experience joy.

"Our eyes should be fixed upon Jesus over anyone else."

Ultimately, it is not being more like others that will make us happy but being more like Christ. Pursuing Christlikeness forms us more and more into the image of Jesus and causes us to become the holy people God created us to be. Being formed into the image of Christ leads to true joy because we are living as God intended and commands. Unless we imitate the walks of faithful believers, any other worldly imitation will keep us from pursuing Christlikeness. Instead of desiring to be like others, our greatest desire should be to be like Jesus.

In John 21:21–22, Peter looks at another disciple and inquires about his fate. Jesus responds by saying, "If I want him to remain until I come ... what is that to you? As for you, follow me." These verses teach us that we should be more consumed with following Jesus than with what other people do. This does not mean we cannot celebrate the successes of others or think about ways to care for and support others, but it does mean that our eyes should be fixed upon Jesus over anyone else. As we follow Jesus, we will learn to embrace how God made us and how He is using our unique qualities for His kingdom's purposes.

ACTION STEP

Consider who you are currently comparing yourself to and desiring to be like. Why do you want to be like this person? How can you reorient these desires to focus on becoming like Jesus instead?

Being formed into the
image of Christ leads to
true joy because we are
living as God intended
and commands.

BIBLIOGRAPHY

Henley, William Ernest. "Invictus." *Poetry Foundation*. The Poetry Foundation. Accessed April 22, 2022. https://www.poetryfoundation.org/poems/51642/invictus.

Thank you for studying
God's Word with us!

CONNECT WITH US
@THEDAILYGRACECO
@DAILYGRACEPODCAST

CONTACT US
INFO@THEDAILYGRACECO.COM

SHARE
#THEDAILYGRACECO

VISIT US ONLINE
WWW.THEDAILYGRACECO.COM

MORE DAILY GRACE
THE DAILY GRACE APP
DAILY GRACE PODCAST

ISBN 979-8-88523-033-9

The Daily *Grace* Co.
— Equipping Disciples in the Word —